In Short, a Memory
of the Other
on a Good Day

In Short, a Memory of the Other on a Good Day

poems by
Allison Cundiff and
Steven Schreiner

Be patient that I address you in a poem,
there is no other
fit medium.
William Carlos Williams

Golden Antelope Press
715 E. McPherson
Kirksville, Missouri 63 501
2014

Copyright ©2014 by Allison Cundiff and Steven Schreiner

All rights reserved. No portion of this publication may be duplicated in any way without the expressed written consent of the publisher, except in the form of brief excerpts or quotations for review purposes.

ISBN   978-1-936135-03-5 (1-936135-03-5)

Library of Congress Control Number: 2014934737

Published by:
Golden Antelope Press
715 E. McPherson
Kirksville, Missouri 63501

Available at:
Golden Antelope Press
715 E. McPherson
Kirksville, Missouri, 63501
Phone: (660) 665-0273
http://www.naciketas-press.com
Email: ndelmoni@gmail.com

For the trust and the pleasure, never one without the other.

Contents

Introduction (Cundiff)	vii
Introduction (Schreiner)	xi
Part One	**1**
Much Better, Schreiner	2
On Writing to Her, Schreiner	3
καρυάτις, Cundiff	4
Break, Cundiff	4
The Call to Prayer, Schreiner	5
The Windows, Cundiff	6
In Response to You Asking If You Should Take A Lover, Schreiner	7
Bidden Moon, Schreiner	7
A Breakup, Cundiff	9
Keith, Cundiff	10
Part Two	**13**
Driving, Cundiff	14
Man on a Stool, Cundiff	14
To Steven / Tell me if this is too much, Cundiff	15
Dancing, Schreiner	17
Just this morning, Cundiff	18
Only A Fool, Schreiner	19
Cover Yourself, Schreiner	20
What is Worse, Schreiner	21

Evie, Cundiff 23
The Wheel of his Bike, Cundiff 25
King and Queen, Schreiner 26

Part Three   29
What a Cunt, Schreiner 30
Alone, Schreiner 31
The Messages, Schreiner 32
Great Ones, Cundiff 33
Some Who Are As We Are, Schreiner 33
I Don't Know, Schreiner 34
Darkroom, Schreiner 35
Breast of A Woman, Cundiff 37
Keatsian, Schreiner 39
You Will Wait, Schreiner 40
You Chose This, Cundiff 43
Talk About the Rain, Schreiner 44
My Father, Cundiff 47
Novinger, MO, Cundiff 49

Part Four   51
to Steven, Cundiff 52
Crossing Missouri, Schreiner 53
Answer me!, Schreiner 55
Bourbon, Cundiff 56
Sister Cristine, Cundiff 57
Never See Her Again, Schreiner 58
Shoveling Snow, Cundiff 59
Love, Schreiner 60
Hands on the Table, Cundiff 63
Bird, Schreiner 64
Easter, 1980, Cundiff 66
Snapshot, Schreiner 68
Because I couldn't believe in a future for us, Schreiner 68
Cliff, Schreiner 70
Bookshelf, Cundiff 71
Dust, Schreiner 71

Dust II, Cundiff	72
You Came Back, Cundiff	73

The Authors   75

Allison Cundiff	76
Steven Schreiner	77

Acknowledgment: "'Much Better' first appeared in *Sukoon Magazine*."

Introduction (Cundiff)

Recently at dinner, a well-meaning friend asked the people at the table why his daughter had to bother with poetry in school. The girl had been asked to analyze a poem, and he couldn't understand how her careful consideration of the color red in one line reflected her ability to think deeply. This man, an engineer, had a point. What does her writing about the color red and what it may or may not connect to have to do with her understanding of human relationships and interaction, her view of the world, her intelligence? She surely could function without thinking of such things. We all could, he argued. I couldn't answer. I thought, though, that the world without thinking of red beyond what it actually is would be, simply, colorless. I suppose this is how he sees red, a less than practical indulgence that deviates from the black and white view of life in function. It is surely a safer way to think, but I am not interested in safety. The world is too much in color, and though I can't say it has made me wealthy or happy, it allows me to feel, and I don't want this to go away.

When Steven and I started writing, friends asked "why bother" with this sort of project. They correctly predicted that nothing "real" would come of it. There would be no marriage between us, and so some couldn't see the point. But do we always need something practical to come of all we do? Isn't the actual impracticality of some things an indicator of their rare and particular place in our worlds? I didn't want a marriage. I wanted companionship in words, and our poems to each other provided that. I learned to be attracted to the hunger that accompanied insatiation. The anticipation of love was more interesting than the love itself, and so we kept our distance. For if we had acted on the words, we would no longer imagine the other. For him, once he said, it was about dipping a toe into the water, just to bring it back out again.

I asked Steven once why we would choose the other to write to. There were years between us, some division of power, our own marriages, and most profoundly, a suffering that bit into each of us deeply. Once he suggested, we provided an earnest audience. Since we were not bound to each other by convention, I could tell him anything, everything, and he would not judge. For some time, I was not able to produce poems if I was not involved with our writing dance. Everything outside of this was duller. The lines blurred and eventually lost their shape. In the absence of longing, there was just the slatewhite bleak. But when we did write, when we were working, there were few other things as honest. We would read carefully what the other wrote. These poems were a defense against loneliness in our locked and self-imposed isolation from the other.

I wish that objects could reflect the intensity of people. He was one of the few men of poetry who didn't terrify me. His stamina for reading was courageous. We would spend an hour on a line and his eyes wouldn't move from the page. His concentrated focus was something I had never seen before. He seemed to understand how a woman wanted to be seen (her fingers when she pushes her hair behind her ear, how she shifts in her seat to cross her leg, the shape of her back when she moves to dress or put on her earrings), how to be touched. And yet he would not expect or demand marriage, children, shared homes. Those, for us, belonged to dead lovers and we did not want to share them again. In the months of the writing, everything was thrown apart. I couldn't hold a cup without thinking of the curve of fingers. But we were calm despite the storm only happening inside. It was big enough to break bones and tear tendons, or so I thought, yet no one needed to know, and our one rule from the day this began was honored: no one was to get hurt.

This is not to say there was not love. I considered myself in love with the small table in his kitchen and the photograph on his mantle and the feel of his books in my hands, his sudden gestures, like how once he came for me so instantly that he was on his knees before me, his face pushing into my sweater and his hands grasping my arms so desperately that I thought, this is it, this is love, this is the gesture that shows it. Not standing at an altar, but a man on his knees on a tile floor, his face on my breast and the way when I looked down I saw his fingers curled around my forearms, my elbows. The thought that even that could have been rehearsed did not occur to me. Could it have been? We might flash recognition at that sort of touch, but we want, as lovers, I think, we want for gestures to be real, the recreated first connections, that we overlook the signs and clutch hope. The shifting eyes are seen and excused, the linger a bit long, an inauthentic word spoken. We ignore everything for our want of authenticity, that first impression.

If we are to put the subject of love aside, this asks us to question what it is that brings us back and back to a single person. What makes us grab keys off a table and leave a dinner on the stove to get to somebody, like I did once, furious, and drove to him, and cried to him in the low summer light of his living room. That night he took my wrist to his lips as I turned to leave him. Or, what makes us lock the doors so our lover cannot get in to us? We think we stay alive for ourselves, but I wonder if that is true. I think we stay alive for the opportunity to love very deeply, very cuttingly, and to perhaps create something from it. All of our walkings and dealings circle around finding love or walking from it, not from making our money or making our bodies comfortable. Our desire to be seen, flaws and all, is what is behind our jobs, our clothes, our many faces, our paychecks, and our errands. That's why I think we should listen carefully to poetry, because we are all in here somewhere too. We can't cut out the red entirely.

I cannot defend the writing and reading of poetry as I am not qualified. I can only say that we must turn to someone or some act of generating beauty or tragedy beyond our immediate practical experience. We feel and suffer and there is too much heaviness in life to ignore color. There has to be something to believe in that is bigger than ourselves. For Steven and me, it has been words.

Introduction (Schreiner)

These poems began in a sandstorm, when Allison and I commenced a conversation across the distance between Kuwait, where I was teaching for a time, and St Louis, where Allison was teaching. They occurred within working days filled with distraction, continued on evenings of too much moonlight, and in time brought us together over wine and talk. We continued writing, even when we could have spoken face to face, inspiring each other, seeking our Muse.

In James Wright's poem "To The Muse," a captivating figure calls to the speaker from the bottom of the Ohio River; each night he leads her back to this world, but each night she returns to the dark. At last he implores her, "Come up to me, Love,/Out of the river, or I will/come down to you." The Muse can't promise fulfillment, only change: Words once more. The end of silence is the Muse's business, and the poet's.

This correspondence in poetry—poems I have written because of Allison, poems Allison has written back—is the occasion we most sought. We speak of all the things we want, and of the things we don't, of parts of the past we trust the other enough to share, of hidden hurts that make us consanguineous. In place of a fixed love, an expectation to be loved, we found these words that deeply connect us to the other. They are literally made of our bodies, and so they become our bodies.

Part One

Much Better, Schreiner

The skin of an apricot
is alive
as a skinned knee a mother must wash,
the raw patch, the tears she loves
and weeps to see and weeps to see
no more, the child grown and reaching
the age of forgetting.
This box of apricots
from Saudi Arabia I lifted up
to my nose and from the golden
dust came the sun
on warm skin. Is it possible
to be as tender as they are,
so that rubbing against one another
as they begin to soften means
some skin comes off as it does from your palm
when you have raked leaves all day?
In the evening, taking your hand
in your hand, or if lucky
in another's hand, see beneath
the peel of us the red membrane
of the scraped knee or the grazed
knuckle as you make supper,
ticklish as the lip to the tip
of another's tongue. But it does not open,
really, until you part it aside
at the seam where it has been sewn
while it played in the wind
on the lifted bough and green waxy leaves.
Isn't it unlike you—how unlikely
after all, to tease an apricot
in the middle of the afternoon
in the workplace 6000 miles
from the woman they remind you of.

On Writing to Her, Schreiner

For fear of preferring this
to all other activities,
aware of her awaiting words,
alert to her in the warm upstairs
of the house at the onset of summer,
now that she is alone, finished
with marriage as one is finished folding
a basket of clean linens
put away unused, not needed, as remote
as a guest room one seldom enters
except when, on the afternoon of a thunderstorm
one opens the door as if a seal on a box
is broken and the contents divulged
new again though familiar, photographs
on the verge of a woods in fall
colors and scent underfoot,
the sweater he loved, how pronounced
her curves, pregnant in the full
season of her love even then
drawn to doubts, the insect buzz
as they walked the warm path
that now she slips behind
another photograph, her favorite,
of her hair drawn back, the look
of fear as if the future had a broken
leg she was about to step down onto ...
what will she need to know
about the second time or the third
that avoids her right now
inducing happiness and vibration
as when her daughter bows the cello?

καρυάτις, Cundiff

Watching you close to sleep,
a clay comfort, your body warm in that space
right before midnight.

You may claim I'm too cold.
"Warm yourself before you touch me,"
you'll say, smiling a little.

I suppose I'm some caryatid
to your earthy Minoan fire.
So I rub my hands together, on my thighs
and then again on your chest.
I want it lasting awhile or to have it over and over.

In those nocturnal pauses,
my crawling towards you as you start to sleep.
You move a bit, an invitation to that space of
baked earth, your body newly comfortable.
And when I match my breasts
to rise and fall with your dark chest
our bodies curled as fronds
and all the silence breathing around us.
The distance of rank and station falls away.

It is almost too much for a woman
with that sound of hide-clad feet against the earth
to take, repeatedly to man's skin.
Where mine is soft, you are hard,
your line for my curve as our shapings
pressing together
their own breathing, their difference.

Break, Cundiff

Our professor gave us a break,
so I went downstairs to get coffee.
He was there, in the shop,

and his sudden tallness,
the lean aloof body, was so
different from the man who shared my bed.
All these weeks I had looked but not looked.
I had to get away, the Bible says,
run away.

He was behind me at the counter,
and we were laughing about the tabouli he bought.
He didn't realize the importance
of a man standing so closely behind me.
Is it terrible to tell you how I brought him back?
back to the cold bed at home?
I used his face and arms.
I wrote a ridiculous poem about it.
Is that what desire is?

Over a month the weather turned from warm to cold,
and he covered his long arms with a sweater
whose cables were like the thin roping muscles there.
I couldn't see his skin move anymore
when he passed by my desk.

The Call to Prayer, Schreiner

The thought that you are still awake, or that you have taken off some article of your clothing, or that your hands are idle, or that you want an apple before bed, or that you put down a book to worry, or that you're looking at a magazine and thinking of new shoes or that the garage needs cleaning or that once, in cut-off shorts, you pressed against a wall at the back of a closet or that you might reach for both posts of the bed before falling asleep and remain like that for a moment opening in the dark or that there's too much homework and this distraction is a nuisance and you intend to say so but when you turn your face aside there's something about your throat that you wish someone would notice or that enough is enough and it's only words and you should be wiser than this and for two days you won't act foolishly just because life is as difficult as always and then on some morning you feel it again and again and try to get to work on time but you don't dare leave the house in that condition inside your clothes.

And then you bring a glass of wine, and one for me, and I think, she's that kind, if you take care of her, despite her appetites, if you tell her it will be okay, no you won't share her, yes you will share her, no she can't touch herself, of course she can touch herself, the kind who won't make you aware of how fucking old you've become, she won't say "it's a shame I did not meet you sooner"; the kind who would serve you first, who would come back after the fight without her lipstick and kiss hunger back to life and leave her clothes on until you're almost the last room of a house fire before it permits only a ruin to remain, something for the rain to piss on, and then over her head comes her sweater, as one changes a child, quickly and filled with experience, and then again her demanding impetuous mouth and her goddam abandon.

The call to prayer sounds again in the empty room where I imprison you; we laugh and blaspheme again. Hold still a moment longer. Surrender your breast to me as to a child. Stop your whimpering.

The Windows, Cundiff

> The windows
> were open and
> all of the world
> outside feigned sleep,
> but I was the honest
> one awake.
> And the cat came by,
> snaking his arched back
> between my calves
> over and over.

In Response to You Asking If You Should Take A Lover, Schreiner

I try not to tell you that my hands look old,
try not to count the years that have passed since we met,
fear that you'll not want me, not nearly as much
as in your memory, that it is
I who want to turn off the voice.
Oh, don't go back to anyone,
not for now,
not even if fire rises from your toes
along your white shins and around the backs of your calves
to the small caves behind your knees
or along your thighs, against the taut cords
that you can feel when you sit upright
and force yourself forward to the front of your chair,
or if your hands drop to your thighs
below your café table and all the young pretty people
are around and it seems like a bad time to feel strict
yet warm at the same time,
what an unwelcome invitation growing along your limbs
and the rivers within or for there to be anything
like the weight of fruit to put your palm to
or that faint rose color where your shirt collar
is two buttons down with three or four more to go
until you're open like a present
for someone who sits on a bed
as you draw near to his face.

Bidden Moon, Schreiner

Then the rain
came in violent
poundings, like someone
beating the months out of a rug.

How long
had it been? Seemed all summer,
a summer of good tomatoes
and dead corn, green husks
but deaf, stunted ears. A summer of killing
the cattle, the ungrazed cattle,
to bring the price down. The clouds came
but the rain hated
to fall, waited to fall, the way
you can hold off the rain for only so long.
I took a woman
to bed, or she took me, as experiment
to see if I could sleep beside someone
again. For some reason
for this woman
I didn't want to say no.
It wasn't sleep. A little hour
fell to her side
or my side of the bed. There was that
waking thing lovers do
again, so long since I'd known it,
when the one stirs against the other
to find she's awake, or ready
to waken. Maybe she lay there
awake in her long comfort
and want, but for
a duration
she neither strayed near
or huffed to a closed shell
guarding her pearl. It was open
the way the moon opens
a room at night
and occupies it. Bidden moon,
would be one way to think of
how I called her
up, forth, me and my

entreaty. And how she held it
against me. How she drained
away after the rain. Why,
she asked me, what could have
possessed you? All her questions
tedious and irksome, all legit,
What do you carry
in your heart; are you good;
according to what standard
are you good; why don't you
look at me? Look at me.

A Breakup, Cundiff

I chose looking at his hands
as our punctuation.
He looked at his watch.

Does time move backwards sometimes?
One mean word from a man I let kiss me, and
I'm unsure, scratching in the jumper from Catholic school.
Seven or maybe twelve and in trouble again.
Can't help it, I'm sorry, I will try harder.
What was his name? Which priest scared me like that.
I can't remember but his face.

Too quickly into this open space,
his bed and beautiful face like
my beagle TicTac was when I let him
suddenly, out of the truck in 1979.
Tic, never leashed,
never left my side but for those days
of the heavy prenoon sky,
too much an American landscape with tall grass,
heavy fields that move bleak blank
when he could have done anything and knew
eyes darting back to me before running off,

my hands weren't the ones that beat him.

So many fields of that tedious childhood
with machines and men
whose eyes were always far away,
the radio scratching when I walked by it, thirsty.

So what is there to do but simply move away,
back away from those fingers
all of them pushing beckoning pressing pressing.

Saying the best words
the worst words when said aloud.
Why do we dive into dark water?
cars full of us diving our bodies dark
like those sketches on the Chauvet cave wall.
That quarry once in college,
following the boys, all with abdomens like my brothers
and surfacing, blue-black water and our faces,
surprising breath.

Keith, Cundiff

I went to visit the barber
whose marble floor and long-abandoned Marvy pole
were the view from my apartment window.
That small town shop hosted spades games every other afternoon
and on Friday nights sometimes.

The country men would bend on creaking knees
to sit on chairs with torn upholstery
you could feel under your clothes.
I sat on an overturned milk crate
smoking Winstons and working on my final paper,
a man named Keith
to my left, and then the barber Larry, whose big tilted window
kept us only a few feet from a sagging street.
A customer would make for after his haircut.

My cat sat in the window of the brick apartment
looking this way and that,
the view his only proof there was an other
outside the place he shared with me.
People on that square moved slower than they do now,
taking their time back to home.

Keith built houses without nails
some sort of Lincoln Logs construction, Larry teased.
He was tall and adolescent lean, his hair grey at the temple.
Larry called me "college girl." Keith called me Allison.

Keith would stand when I came in the door.
Quiet during the games, but smiling.
His handwriting keeping score,
showing he stopped school at 14.

He walked me to my apartment door after every game.
He always won against me and Larry
but gave me my waitressing tips back in his cool fingers.
My apartment steps were in the alley, and in the dark his
    mouth would say,
"It's not safe for a lady to walk alone."

A lady I thought. I was 19.
I went back to the shop last week to visit.
I had stayed away too many years, I knew.
Before the jingle of the door had stopped
Larry knew me.
And he told me.

Keith had killed himself,
"cause of money problems,"
he said.

The floor's black tiles
had faded to slate.
I sat down by the window again, the same crates there.
The backwards B was always blocked by Keith,
but I could see it now through the empty.
The tear in the chair wider after twenty years.

If I close my eyes I see him again,
how a body holds a shape under a shirt?
And mine too, younger.

Part Two

Driving, Cundiff

In the backseat of my car
a stranger driving
and we seem to hug the curb too much.
The vodka burning through my dress.
and I almost feel you warm between my ribcage
spreading dark webs
under my sternum
milking through inside vessels
your inky finger reaching down
over belly hunger, hooking
the bold wide bone of my pelvis
under your weight
curling inside the slipping space
and I reluctantly open
my knees
two red circles suddenly cold
where my skin pressed
together just before
sudden twin ovals
two minutes from gone.
And the road clears
straight again and you are
gone, where I'm used to you being.

Man on a Stool, Cundiff

On a stool at the bar he waited.
And when I walked up behind him there was
a space
before he saw me, his eyes latching onto
some elsewhere.
Felt like hiding and not yet found
if just for a moment again
in a child's game.

Poets are dangerous.
They turn us over and look at everything
on our bellies.
I keep trying to right my weight.

He sees what's wrong about me,
those reasons I became quiet all that time ago.
Someone who would rest her chin
on the forearm halfway through the car window.
"Don't put your hand out the window on the road!"
they'd say.
I didn't understand why they cared so much for careful.
Same reason why adults won't swim when they grow up.

Bodies are haunting when they first come
and then again when they go.
First the sudden bloated shock of a face.
I kissed those lips,
they match, here on my breast.
The brow again,
it furrowed (he wanted me to lie back),
His hands on a drink,
moving to greet me again.
This time they weren't against my shoulder,
his palm grazing the slope of my breast
again and again.

To Steven / Tell me if this is too much, Cundiff

I've stopped by the market again.
Living paycheck to paycheck
makes for smaller meals
and more stops for little items.
The farmers have come to know
my strange face finally.

An older woman offered me
something smoked from her plate.

She sat in her little tent
surrounded by hanging peppers,
more pears than anyone could count,
and burlap sacks of mystery bulgings.
Her dish was dark,
fresh and otherworldly.
This piece had a life somewhere
before my mouth, the sea
or with adrenaline, running from
all those things wanting to kill it.

It reminded me of how I might taste
shocking and familiar
to myself, on your lips.
If you've been down on me,
which I can barely take,
moving too much in pleasure,
I always try to make quiet.
Then please kiss me,
since from your mouth, its comfort
and heat, the spice there.
A strange marriage of mystery
from its corners.

Dancing, Schreiner

From all the places on the earth
Where the sea has been
What then if one of those places
Is you, or in you
When one has been to Gibraltar
And Portugal, when one has been all night
Dancing in a dive with lifted arms
And rising blouse
Over the damnedest sights
One has beheld
Signaling, O, signaling
Not the end but the Origin
And not the last of the evening
To touch her
As the last lingering waves of her perfume
Are not the last lingering waves
But only that scent
To be altered by that scent
That she gives off in heat
What then what then all you cunts
And all you cocks
What then should you say
And to whom will you say
What you know you won't say
And what a blessing not to want
To say it or need to say it,
That a man knelt down to you before you came home
And your hands—what will you do, cut them off!?—
Were part of the urgency
With which you literally
Galloped upon the shores of his prayer
And then dragged him the length of you
The whole field of you trampled
By lust

So that you were barely alive
When you pushed your mouth burned from
I know you remember what, burned and wanting
It again and again to swell between your adagio
Lips, you and your slow mount,
You and your casual star turn,
To taste yourself
And then to wear that perfume home,
What of it?

Just this morning, Cundiff

Don't bend over, you said.
Funny, I thought, at that moment,
the supple act of bending.

I bent to watch my fingers
move across my ankle
to strap on my sandal last summer.
Like bending to kiss down your back.
Like long morning stretches
when images suddenly come back
even though you didn't call them to you.

Fingers bend too
in so many places
one in my mouth
inside yours then
which is more the wet or warm.
your thumb touching my chin
while I watch you feeding me a fig.
I want to feed you
feed on you.
looking up at you from below.

Just this morning again
that hunger came,
it won't listen,

comes in the worst of times.
This morning as I sat on the edge of the tub
shaving my leg, bending,
same ankle up, the ankle
you put in your hand once
and looked at like you might
a handful of new fruit at the market.

The porcelain is cold under me.
In my hand a razor,
I must be more careful.

Only A Fool, Schreiner

There is, too, the suggestion of assertiveness
About you. Or would only a fool
Call it a suggestion? Last week on one night
Alone you broke off with your lover, took another,
Visited the biker bar again, met me
For a drink, wore your hair in a pile atop your head
And falling on occasion across your face, let
A certain smile suffuse your face
Each time you reminded me—why not just say
What you said, you had been in love
With me—and when the window, your
Word, was over, as it had been open
And I came to you through it and you
Came to me through it, and you had prepared
Yourself, any fool could see you had more than
Your child's cello lesson in mind, could see the intent
Of my martini as it worked its way up the side of my throat
And as your tight clothes seemed to urge
You out of them, the light just right in the place
You had picked, for your little innocent glass of wine
And your thoughtful smile and the storm brewing
In your hair, and your endless legs needing more

Than space below the table allowed
So you swung them this way or that, how
I enjoyed watching the safety you had proclaimed for your-
    self
And the reasons you had for keeping still
Being violated by me, oh how I enjoyed the rain
That kept falling so that we had to run
To your car closer than mine and how once inside
In your bucket seats split by the assertive stick shift
You knew, you knew that you could:
Telling me to take a lover, laughing without derision,
Making me ask once again for another
Parting kiss.

Cover Yourself, Schreiner

If I told you to cover up
Because there should never be nakedness
Like yours, nor confidence nor amplitude
Nor matching parts or lengths of rope
Across a body nor ribbons such as I keep
In my drawer, broad bands of grosgrain ribbons
For when I might have a lover or on some night may want
To feel like a gift and so will tie myself
The way Joe Dallesandro did once in that first Warhol movie
I went to The Village to watch as a troubled teen ...
My own waiting as though someone else
Were in the bed or soon to be,
—didn't you ever do anything you were ashamed of
Until you met someone you could tell
Was not ashamed for you but thoughtful—
I must have meant, Don't cover up, don't hide
Yourself from me, don't reveal everything tonight but
Don't hide from me. Don't confuse me
With someone else from whom you have no need
To be shy any longer. For what I intend

To do to you
You need to be discrete, to wait
As one waits in the rain outside the window
Of one who broke her heart, getting
Wetter and wetter
And still not going home.

What is Worse, Schreiner

because you had written that showing a portion of your breast did not mean you were to be taken ...

First there is the length of you
but that is obvious. And there are
the hours and hours of a child's first pleasure.
Do you think it is unseemly of me to drink like that?

Have you thought much about your ears
as more than a porch to pour my words,
you Shakespearian hussy, or windows where
imprints of my kisses fly like insults?

What about the place where your shoulder meets
your breastbone, like a wing, hollow
underneath, dark with a deep depression
and scented like a field where something wild

has fallen and will soon be approached
to be skinned. What goes there
is never talked about, until your arms
are pinned above your head to the bedstead

of wood, burning girl. You don't think I could find
something to do to you there? You think anything
is offputting? I don't even discuss
what forms the front gate to your entrance

because your mouth is what I'm given. Enough
to know that I have pried open there

all the secrets of your silence; have seen you
gasp as if for air, kiss as if you had to spill

what pooled there against your will.
That time just after childhood when something hard
began to occur, the tightening of your muscles
as if you kept a clutch of eggs between your legs

and clenching like that you felt dizzy and eruptive
as when a firecracker goes off in the hand.
And boys and men began to look at you
even when you didn't have your back turned. So you looked
    back,

too. All that's over now. There are worse things
and I am one of them. I don't know when it first occurred
to me that what I wanted to do to a woman, or a girl
soon to be a woman or do what makes a girl a woman,

was to take her love, to make her love me
and to take her love, to trade it for desire
which is a way to take everything she has
and leave her nothing except more want.

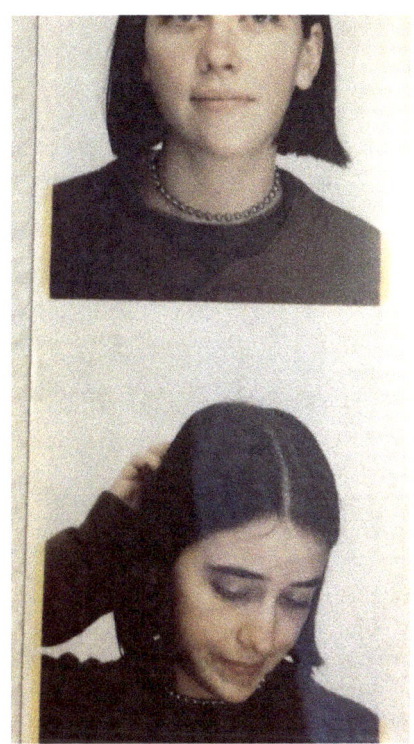

Evie, Cundiff

I had a doppelganger in college, Evie.
We were both English majors.
She went to South America to study, I went to Ireland.
She was my neighbor junior year
after what happenedtome happenedtome,
it happened to her too. Don't talk about it,
don't tell because, and do you know,
if you don't talk it goes away? it goes away
just DON'T fucking ask, okay.

Like cigarette rings we practiced to make so good.
but hers were red lines around her eyelids
shaking, scary when she slept.

She was so mad,
so she gathered all the coffee cups she could find.
through the halls, her flat feet and straw-man hair down her
    back,
knocking on each door in Miller Apartments.
And with her hands fullfulloverfull with coffee cups all kinds
    of colors,
(there was a green one green like my eyes she said and she
    gave that one
to me) people just gave them over to her!
She came to my house next door.
I had the cat in my arms.
I have a picture of her that night.
We took these cups, mounds of them, falling, our faces laugh-
    ing
our mouths in shapes of O's
to the brick behind her apartment,
my feet wet in my shoes from the outside
and we threw them one after the other,
our skinny ivory arms at the brick
and laughing laughing all those pieces,
shrapnel coming everywhere.

Evie and I would go out once a semester
or so and find a beautiful poet-looking boy.
And the two of us would descend on him.
He would always come back with us,
always to her place,
never mine.

And after
she would stay and clear the cups, and I would walk him
    home.
Was that my body?

Evie came back from Bolivia with malaria,
and I spoon-fed her broth
from a coffee cup.

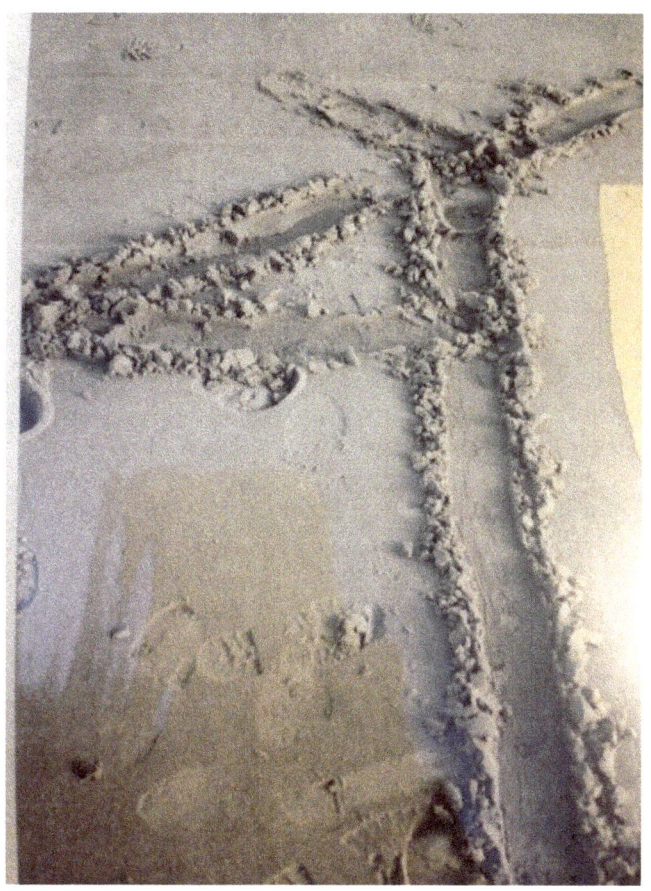

The Wheel of his Bike, Cundiff

There was a boy Beth and I trusted,
he grew up in a cold house near me,
rode his bike over, dismissed it on its side
in the lawn next to the beagle pups and snow plow,
the back wheel spinning an arc of silver clicks.

We had licked the blood
off each other's cuts,

and he held my sweating hair off my neck
so I could drink from a public fountain.
So when he turned to me
on one of the last days of August,
four days before Beth turned 16
when all the heaviness of school was soon,
and said, "kiss her,"
I did.

Beth's eyes were closed hard enough
when I leaned close. Close enough to see
opaque hairs on her cheeks.
"It's soft," she said.
"More than a boy's."

And after she sat looking up at a summer sky
pushing her lips back and forth,
I stared at him, hard,
thinking how good it felt
to obey a boy I knew.
The way the water darkened his hair in the lake,
when he surfaced for breath,
which we all do when kissing,
and how when he raced against me on concrete sidewalks,
a genuine companion,
I shouted "wait,"
bent in loss behind the finish line, my belly in a knot
of safe defeat.

And he would stop for me.
I threw grass at his face, laughing,
before we grew into some impossible difference.

King and Queen, Schreiner

What if greatness were found
in just a woman's body? And her
proportions a thing by which

we might be ruled? It will bore you
that I begin with your breasts; we've had this
discussion before: how easy it is to ignore
what guarantees satisfaction. I think Chagall
adored Bella's breasts; though he made them round
to suggest their perfection,
he always adorned her like a bride. Himself
he painted as variously a juggler
horseman acrobat horse
or courtier. It's dangerous to place a beast
on the ceiling, to find a rooster in the sky,
and green signified his delight
to have encountered beauty where love
was required. I don't paint
but that night with your torso turned
aside and your breast risen in candle
smoke I wondered what effect
pregnancy had on you, whether your milk
had never let down, whether it flowed
as from twin fountains, why they seemed in-
exhaustible. It was true there was something boyish
about you, if voluptuary boys might serve the delight
of the king you made me. Why had you been naked
in that parting light, if not to suggest careless
arrogance? You are forgiven
for not particularly wanting me
to nurse.
As you taper toward the waist
and flare as is best, as you ride out to sea
on the ship of your hips, as you lengthen
toward the knee and curve at the stern
keel of your back, as you sway and close
like a shell under the sea, as my hands
pass over your clean endings, as I would bend
to open you as one raises a hatch in the dark
of the ship, as one with strong hands halves

an apple that has been partly
split with the thin seam made by a
fingernail, I might bring you down
to the ground where you must lay,
as one does to animals called trophies
because they are great but great only in that one's
mind who has earned submission. Thus
parted and supine, still rippling
as when wind courses through the window
and over the spine, the small hairs there and all the nerves
wiser and surer made certain by desire,
you may rule your kingdom
and your king.

Part Three

What a Cunt, Schreiner

should be: private
and inviolate, slightly
forward, revolved toward
the stars and moon, underneath
everything she is, always
walking within her, yes
the lips may be slightly parted
as lips are in thirst,
and pink, able to flow
with its own waters
like a well, or to be closed
and forbidden, not to be
touched, unless by fingertips
delicate enough to pick out
lentils or diamonds or sapphires
bedded in the dust
lift them and drop them
into a velvet pouch
It should be secret
all day long
all night long too
if need be
if no one arrives
as sometimes no one does
at the lip of the sea
so it goes untouched
not entered from dry land
yet beating and whispering
against the shore
and sometimes when it rages
rising up as if out of sleep
to take something back
to a place unseen
it alone decides

what to do with possession
rarely, if ever, leaving one
the same
who has been
embraced
in its waters
and waves

Alone, Schreiner

Alone at midnight
in this world lit by a white lie

which means the moon
is full

as you are full
there floats a ghost

of doubt
who comes over you

as the night
and covers you like a gown

undressed and ready
for your new lover

how odd
to be this alone

at such an hour
inimical to love

what speaks to you
is not desire no longer sharp

and formidable
but a gaping

and trenchant awakeness
made unpleasant by absence

yes you love
yes you gave

yes you want
wanted and received

yes you revived love
in another yes you lost

what you loved
yes you soared

and inspired just by
walking back and forth

like a tiger
tonight the moon betrays you

alone and alone
as if you did not exist.

The Messages, Schreiner

the messages
we sent
had no content
as promised
so to each other

for the sake of space
and opportunity
we gave cold comfort
which did and did not
suffice. shall I tell you
what it feels like
to be placed side by side
in a cold sky
while the days and nights pass?
during the day while the sun
brightens and declines
and business takes place

and clothes are worn
and love anticipated
it is easy to wish one well
because as the night approaches
one imagines great new
events of love soon to occur
so the feeling of freedom
freedom from domination
no matter how desired
allows us side by side
to think of shining
and stirring the hearts of others
but in the day invisible like that
should come the knowledge
that night only reveals
how the brightnesses
shine alone and are alone

Great Ones, Cundiff

Then the great loves of our lives
standing between us
and every single date.

Their ancient presence like
a towerhigh desert statue
to be revisited every day.

The dry sameness of their sandy fingers
when in my hand shatters into a million pieces.

Some Who Are As We Are, Schreiner

Is it possible some, who
are as we are, know love
too well and therefore not
at all?

have we not wanted it
more than anything, only to find
it difficult and elusive, for
which we can only blame
ourselves? has it been the
fault of wanting? Is there
such a thing as love greed?
I have to think that
at the heart of hunger lies some kind
of hurt, just as
at the heart of distance
lies that same hurt.
I have always been
fascinated by the fact
that a star might
be dead!
a different love is
the love for a child.
here too parents
make mistakes
or perhaps correct them.

I Don't Know, Schreiner

yes I would like to
be well

and yes
i don't know why i hurried
or acted so eager
to take off my shirt
i still think of that dim light
in my room where you
reached
behind you with your hands like that
all those years of practice

and i did nothing to stop you
as you came undone
and later when
the tentative
was over with
i led your hand to me
yes
next time
time will be much slower
and take much longer
you will need to learn
as if being taught
when to do nothing
how to be still
whether to stir
where to swim with your
limbs
what the words want to say
what the mouth is for

Darkroom, Schreiner

That rain is falling,
that rain we always talk about
that never falls on us.
I see you with your skirt hiked up
with your sandals in your hand
to avoid getting wet in the deep puddles.
Or maybe you are playing
with the rain
running down your face and your arms
and dragging your hair down, weighing
as water will
heavy on your clothes. Your shirt
is a man's dress shirt you kept
when your lover died

and which you wear like Georgia
O'Keefe waiting for Alfred Stieglitz
to arrive from his city
to her Pueblo. She's been painting
in a wide hat; he's been dodging taxis
in the dark Manhattan evening
on a day that revealed
only black and white figures
swimming up to him from the chemical baths
of his darkroom. With the red light on
everything was smoke, as in war.
All day the sun stood by her, her only true
lover, and lit the calyx of her lily.
What large petals, and what a demented,
pollinated stamen among the swelling sepals.
Then the bone-white afterlife
she sought in a skull. What has this
to do with you, or the rain?
It's just that, when I was away
in my lonely, vexed vigil
to my mother's late flowering
I was unable, it felt, to touch
anything—not the past, not you, not
myself. I so wanted to be awakened
by beauty or stirred by desire
instead of anguished and cold,
unlike after a death
when one is bereft and maddened
with urge, the great, unfulfillable
hunger after the end. This, this
state I was in, was all prelude
filled with ire and the insistence
to remember to be kind that one must practice
constantly among the frightened, greedy
dying. So it was that I imagined
because I could not touch anything

(nightly I simply sat in a dark room
I returned to after she had been put to bed,
letting the phone emit this or that
message, yes one was yours, no one was not ...)
that I wanted to approach you
but not touch you, not permit you
to reach for me, not take off what
had gotten wet, not fall upon one
another as lovers do who've been apart
when they meet on an all-afternoon rain
but to stand beside you in the sunlight
that strips away everything we are, leaving
either a wet, willing flower's mouth
or a bleached, wide-eyed death's head.

Breast of A Woman, Cundiff

The breast of a woman
may hold so many objects:
The profile weight of a cat,
that vulnerable purring
against one's own rhythms.
Or a child's occasional and
sudden weight, crashing in
then leaving, or heavy
there but sweet, that
temporary small love so
you never move her, keep
her still, little hands on
your neck, little breath.

Then the other, the hands
of a lover
less gentle.
How to hold
a nipple expertly between

two slender fingers
her mouth parted so that the skin in the
corners still connects.

Then the man,
his distant face always eyeing the sea.
God's face,
don't go, I said to one
and he never did.
but then I did.
I was ripped away by that same sea
and my father.
One plane can do a lot of damage to love.

I asked a friend, why love you?
Yet Odysseus reached for Anticlea in Hades,
though she wisped away.
It was the reaching
that made him great.

Would I ever tell another I am
worthy of his ancient
or doomed love?
Would I dare say to you,
bring me
close enough to whisper without shame,
smile full on right to my face.
It may end.
Let me see you outside of your mystery.
Believe in me.
I can't promise not to leave
I can't promise that lover
won't have the standard of Keats'
lover on the urn to compete with,
but forget all that.
Touch me in the morning before our eyes are open.
push yourself urgently inside after I climb
on top, as though

you cannot bear to take the
time to make me wet,
but then you quickly finish
when you realize I already was,
that perfect male surprise.

Keatsian, Schreiner

If it should happen
In an hour of the evening
Devoted to study and its tireless
Preparation while seated in the places
Designed for serious friends
With a glass of wine to ease
The awful dark of Sunday evening
With its harrowing promise of waking
And rising to begin the school week
Which as children we accepted
And as teachers we endure,
While above us the children
Emerge from childhood still so in need
Of protection,
That I should notice your difficulty
To concentrate or see your flightless
Fingers surround a goblet glowing
Red and warm, fingers I've felt
Discern just the right pressure to apply
As one must decide what to do next
With a trapped bird and reaching to it
Can't equilibrate the pulse there
Of a force in feathers
With the power of a grip's significant
Strength, then does at once so accurately
As to betray experience with trapped things
And the want of release; if you see
Me looking at your hands like that

As the hour passes and the wine drains
As from a desk a task is erased
As the clock gains and loses
By its steady ignorance of desire,
Or if your mouth should open to say
Words I don't question
About the tendency of visits
To end, or if because you knew
You would be caught in compromise
And I intend to make you complicit
That you wore that particular
Whatever it was you wore that day
With forethought, it's too late
For all that thoughtful folding
And unfolding of your limbs.
You'll know when I've gone
What you're left with and what
Still needs to be done.

You Will Wait, Schreiner

There are days of course
when one feels the muchness
of waiting. This is good practice. A woman
may intend a man to wait. She prepares
her hair or the look of her mouth,
and she applies care to her eyes
which are either locked or unlocked.
Students are taught to wait by the sheer
ennui of afternoon, the dragging last class
in which the Spanish teacher, herself bored
and young, slender and heavy with desire
for a night when she will be loved
perhaps roughly and then comforted
by the mutual cry she and her lover attain so full
of forgetting, so foreign and untranslatable,

sees a boy who has grown too tall
too strong and too aware
yawn, so that she yawns, smiles, forgives
herself for what she has aspired to
in her waiting. Wait wait wait
thinks the man. Give in to time.
After all, you have waited while she pulled up
the hem of her blouse, even if she seemed hasty
to be made an example of: for what else
is a woman who has removed the layers
between her body and another but
an example: here is her choice of silk
and here is how she thought of herself
this morning when she pulled the straps
over her shoulders and then drew down
a sweater, smooth and profound
as a perfect audition; what else should she be
but an example of how one steps free
from the foolish little proof that
she has perfected her innocence
by not showing what is hidden
until some thin fingers pull aside an insubstantial
subterfuge: I am dressed. *Undress me.*
And of course no one enters there
without a lengthy wait which of itself
is prelude to invitation or rejection,
therefore more waiting. And all this occurs
early in the dawn light in the warm room
when her legs begin to disappear in skirt
and boots, and what are boots but more
waiting, which is what a skirt is if you ask
any lover.
        Imagine a woman in a skirt
to a woman in a skirt, both having worked
the long week until the end; why else
come Friday night in a dim lit danger

of bar talk and thirst does she thrust
out her dollars and walk to her car
and drive across the state line
dark in doubt and tasting a mouth
she's never tasted before. The hours she waits
are reason enough
to let the other savage her. Not enough
waiting. Not enough, I tell you. You must learn
how long it takes
as it rises along your thighs or spirals
from the tips of your fingers
into your daunting recesses. If I darken
the mouth of your breast with my mouth,
if you taste the lips of your taste on my lips,
it is only because you have waited. But you have to
wait longer than you even have lived.
The day when you are displayed as if for a lesson
with your arms above your head
not your arms any longer, not free to move them
to your sides or with your fingers
to hold me there
at some edge of emergence, moving through you
some uprising as from hidden streams
after rain has swelled them and they crash
through trees out of nowhere, try moving
your head side to side, sluicing through the pillow
with your hair on fire
or if you are turned over as one turns a body pulled
from a fire over until it lies still, stop writhing
when your furrowed back is exposed
as though for whipping and stop raising up
your rump, it's all the same, don't push yourself
against the sheet between your legs, stop rustling
like leaves in the breeze, stop twisting your hands
free, the knots will come undone
long after you've come undone, long after you've given up

waiting which, now that you're without decency
as one is without secrets, as you are without
your outfit and your calculations,
you will wait.

You Chose This, Cundiff

You chose this for yourself, didn't you?
Nothing has happened to you
that wasn't done to you, done to that one too.
Or maybe you woke up to breakfast cereal like every other
   one of us
and decided you'd rather just starve.
You'd be too
old, too fucked up, too attached to one before, too hurt.
Do you play at that? These are the things
that people do to one another.

Last summer the sheets were cold, the room morning black
and the palm of my hand rested against my right hip bone,
jutting forward like some branch from hard earth.
Hips hold many objects. That space is perfect for a baby,
a bag of flour maybe, were I some village girl.
And if I were, I thought, a village girl,
would you have me then? I'd be brown and scrappy,
my hair in braids, my breasts bare.
I'd make excuses to be in your yard suddenly,
maybe gathering firewood.
You'd still be older, shoo me away,
"You're too romantic," you'd say all furrow and gristle.
I would laugh at you and go.

Last summer I would sleep to the sound of the cicadas
rubbing shells, proboscis pushing
against my white window.
Your poem hidden on my wall next to my bed.
Remember when I slept against you,

your fingers tucked around my everyday sheets?
You let me push my breasts into your back.
"Don't worry," I whispered.
You repeated, "You really don't want anything more from me
    than this?"
Just to be invisibly tucked behind you,
the safety of men, the danger of that safety.

Last summer I walked from you and
my feet left prints in the cool sawdust.
I climbed onto a chair to reach up
for the book I had hidden, on the tips of my dirty toes.
That book with the sketches of the hawk,
the hawk I saw circle my backyard
as I stood with the baby on my hip,
all your angles still in the line of the bird,
the arm you held out to push away with,
under my skin, under my nails.

Talk About the Rain, Schreiner

And yes the words
themselves are great
until they gather and appear
like this morning's storm
and are massed against us
just what have they
against us
I don't mind saying
that today my body
feels heavy and weighted
freighted as though
carrying something
intended for you
which is to say I
am not full

of the indifference you despise
nor of restraint
that I feel the falling
of the rain the constant thud
of thunder against the sky
as you slept through dawn
under the breaths
of the dogs
was my change
my weather

midnight began to betray
a difficult feeling
made of words
for which there were no words
your reply to my reply
your rebuke of my rebuke
the way one answers
what have you done
by saying the same thing
what have you done
the reassessment
of virtues one thought
commendable in restraint
the reassignment of blame
make me a woman
make me want
and not attain make me hurt
as when I stiffen
like a child refusing
the vaccine

it will seem that you have been watered
by this change
that I am storming
over your house
sluicing through your garden
trailing like a vine

down the glass pane
that I want in
even under the soles
of your elegant boots
or that I am the drop
that surprises you
against your neck
on your back
or your eyelid
when your hair almost dry
reminds you
that under all your protection
you were naked
a moment ago

but it isn't so really
it isn't so
this rain will stop
always always ceases
need turns to flood
as after drought
the ground hardens again
what was it you said
satiety and intimacy
as though you were quoting
how last night's symphony
fell upon you
well the rain falls
the rain stops
I like that about the rain

My Father, Cundiff

When my father was not yet forty,
my own age now,
his eyes stayed far away
behind the wheel of the Ford tractor
or the barrel of the ribbed brown gun
that leaned against the back wall of the closet
when not hanging in his arm,
while he followed the beagle we loved.

That closet door faced west.
I took two breaths before I turned the handle.
That gun he placed in my arms,
the crosshairs darker indoors.

The gun is now gone to my brother's closet.
New dogs follow me back indoors.
I drive but do not see the road.

The head of my bed faces east.
The foot of your bed reaches north.
and lying there, you lift my wrists south.
This woman asked me,
where do you go to when your eyes go far away?

Novinger, MO, Cundiff

there were four cans lined up on that hollowed mossy log
that had always been there it seemed
and we stood before it not talking the other woman and I,
quiet aside the men not because they made us
but because they would not hurt us we knew
and sometimes when men talk evenly
and they are all the same with beautiful shoulders
and denim cuffs over boots that have been resoled
and drops of paint dried on top
but those are the shoes they wore after work too.
and I had brought cold lunch for the hunters
but it was nearing sunset and the sweet feeling
of cooking for a really good man,
one who would grow to love me back,
oh but love at 19 was looking up and catching,
seeing his pain as he saw the run in my tights
or the too young face he shamed himself for loving.
and they all had guns
their fathers had taught them to shoot
and I held my boss's baby
whose teeth were aching and my pinky finger in his mouth
all those pink ridges, poor thing,
and judy had the toddler who kicked her belly with his boots
and the beer was in a can in my lover's brown fingers.
and all I could have been was there at that log,
a good man's wife,
my belly taut and sweetly pregnant over and over
too young, making love over and over to a man
who wouldn't have squinted his eyes shut
and instead would put his hand on the small of my back
ohgod a man's hand there.
A man who smiled when he pulled inside of me,
as to say, this is right, no one is getting hurt,
I know this woman loves me. I'll smile with crooked teeth

and know she will think me beautiful.

I was behind with the reading for class
but said yes so I could help just with the babies
while the men of course had guns but in my backseat
I kept a notebook and once he asked,
did I write about him?
and I told him, baby, I have poems about you
but I won't show you till you keep your promise
to take me on that motorcycle to the desert
where you'll hold my cold burned skin
in some tent and his eyes were blue
and he was taller than me and he looked down then
but a good Catholic girl can't give those things away completely.
and his hands were tired after a day,
deep occasional cuts through coarse skin.
You know the shaking like the Elgar cello concerto opening chords?

I won't talk about the falling away,
but I want to tell you that once
on a thursday sunset,
I handed over a teething baby
to his mother, lifted a rifle to my cheek,
and shot off two cans from a log in Novinger
under the eye of a hunter
eating the cold dinner I had made him,
his hand low on my back to steady my aim.

Part Four

to Steven, Cundiff

> Standing outside your window,
> I can just make out blurrings of your arms
> shading the corners of your room.
>
> It's raining again, and the sharpness of
> your body inside is sinking dread,
> without mine pressing behind you.
>
> What if I were to bare my breast to you?

You would be unmoved, still perched on your cold rock,
your siren fingers holding you steady.

I try, but can't push my desire down deep enough under the cold soil.

A perfect place would be in a garden grave of a friend
whose herbs in winter curl inside themselves below a broad window.

Wanting you should be allowed to be bigger.
Heavy like the sudden slow standing of large animals
upon ice, finally. But you are always always still.
Never moved. Even when I reach out for your shoulder,
feeling for the angles there, where the muscles move your hand to write.

In the morning light the objects in your house had shifted.
The books stacked were heavier, the texture of a quilt had your
footsteps in it.
The small considerations of your cups, your cutting board,
even the broad window where, just before, I had stood below.

Crossing Missouri, Schreiner

You were driving.
Crossing Missouri
down out of Kansas City
and into the windy landscape
a devouring kind of width
under a sky closing in
that would only get tighter
and narrower like a passage
a river has to make
into another wider body
before releasing into namelessness
and no longer what it was
even to itself. Erase me

and you find much the same.
In this I am unlike that river
or like that river
when it has spilled over
the way yesterday the Meramec
flowed where a child and I
walked and hunted imagined
creatures. He saw the ghost
high in the sky wearing white
where the trees were zombie
green. I wanted to return
to a promise we had talked
about, you and I. This came first
this boy, this imaginary
forest, the danger dwelling
in the next ravine. Rainwater
and runoff and nothing with will
made the flood
and would soon be gone
into the ground
into the river
under the sea. I wanted
you but understood
how my returning
was like your returning
to difficulties and masks.
You were driving home
the fields empty
a beam of sun weighed against
your thigh, a belt crossed
over your shoulder holding you
back. Your long fingers held
the black wheel, the phone
rested against leather.
You no more wanted
to have your trip end

than I wanted to have to make
a stick a sword
a branch a snake
a ditch full of water
a flood. I should have thought
by now you'd turn
to another, even a task
will take that place,
but in my mind
you are driving
and telling me you are going
to see me again
do this again
and I am saying Please
Please Please Please
don't and you are doing 70
and you are saying Yes
Yes you will.

Answer me!, Schreiner

Answer me, who have no right
to ask or to insist. Answer
with your breath
or your hair turning like a storm
at night over me.
Answer me with the way you take off
your shoes, stepping out of them
as if falling a few inches
into the meaning of home
or into an intention
to go on undoing the day
and all it has been to you, friend
and occupant, enemy from afar
sending shells into your neighborhood.
Take off your clothes

as though you were walking outside
in the rain; did you really mean to
undress in front of me, to say you wished
to be that way again, only this time
that you wanted to go even further
into my embrace? I ask
because I have been assaulted
by the same strange wish, to be naked
against you, to be under the spell
of daylight in front of you
as though it were night and we lovers
again, this time with a conviction
to go to our destruction
fighting for the same side.

Bourbon, Cundiff

Sometimes what beckons
is the bleakness of a city street,
the industrial block with clips
of sudden white graffiti by opaque cubed
windows and fences that I shamefully thought
looked like cum and with machines
and my body lost between
all these abandoned parts,
the way Beth and I snuck here
as girls my legs were always so long,
skinny before womanhood,
looking as we all did who hadn't been hurt
yet longed to be hurt a little.
Sitting on top of city trains
whose immense blackness
had the power to crush us
but sat silently under our thighs in the darkness,
we passed between us
bourbon I stole from my mother.

Sister Cristine, Cundiff

    You have to know though
    I was once capable of innocence.
    It was like wearing a heavy robe.
    I'd see the public school girls laughing,
    all teeth, while my lips and legs pressed
    together under the lined paper.
    I had to seek out boys to touch me.

It was always too easy,
their eyes locked on my small breasts, on their own hands
between my legs.

The sisters would walk us to church on Wednesdays.
The incense and their hands raised, the fingers on the pews
   ahead of them,
The beauty of kneeling. His long suffering body, the sting in
   his eyes from the crown.
I was in love with God, had dreams about his height, the tunic
   he wore

And then back in school, next to the church, the nuns' angular chins and their chalked fingers. It was too terrifying to raise our hands to ask permission to use the restroom, Sister, no not can, may I? No, not yet. So we wet ourselves against the firm film of wood base of the desks. I prayed the itching wool of my skirt would catch the wetness instead of my skin. Prayed for the poor souls in purgatory, prayed for the saints and their beautiful skin, eyes like St. Teresa turned in adoration to Christ, prayed for my parents, the 13 puppies in the backyard with the 12 nursing stations, prayed my father would give me the runt instead of shoot him, and he did. We named him Tic tac. Sister Cristine took me by the elbow, and her breath on my lip like a long absent sister, whispered, here, her black habit on a woman's legs, helping me with urine soaked panties, this small kindness, and helped me slip into clean white cotton underwear, the whole time, me thinking, whose were these? Who will wash mine? And don't tell my father, *of course not sweetheart, there there.*

Never See Her Again, Schreiner

I thought, What a good thing
she's gone, you can go
to the doctor, you can go to the Y,
you can change the oil
ride your motorcycle
look at the nearly naked
women in the swimsuit issue

like a boy. You can hear the birds
and the sincere, if indecisive, cardinal
calling to his dull mate.
But you can't
read that deranged poet, Anna
Akhmatova, her insane demands
that love never betray her.
You can't drink your single malt
without having to sting
this woman, off to Kisstown
and Touchland
wearing her hair in a tornado
knowing that her earrings,
the large silver hoops impossibly
light and round and gigantic
which she took off to take you
to bed,
are here in an envelope with her name,
her first and last name,
written in your childish purple ink
as if you were going to forget
whose they were, as if you were going
to address them to her
mail them to her
never see her again.

Shoveling Snow, Cundiff

The little boy across the street
ran up hard to my leg yesterday.
He wore a superman cape
on the outside of his coat.
He has worn it for two years now.
He helped me shovel show
by walking in front of me
and singing something from his mind

and the red of his cape dark at the tips.

His mother was inside
and she asked us to keep an eye
so my daughter lifted him
as she might her own child.
The boys ran inside
for the hiding cat again to put him in the snow.
And in the noise of our laughter
the sound I missed most
was your voice in casual mention
of coffee gone cold or
the reading of that article,
your accent still stuck to your words
on the surprising delight of a snow day.

And in the city last week
I pressed against a building to keep warm
I knew I was close to Benton Park,
I felt you in the meat shop
with the men all around,
I smelled you next door in the spice shop.
I asked, they don't have cloves.
That's your kiss, that's what I smoked wrapped
in grape leaves in college,
that's what happens before noon on a Saturday
when I think of you.
I wander into spice shops.
I bump into people
and have to say sorry.

Love, Schreiner

not a full day no but
something of a moment
something in pajamas
something insistent

consistent and concerned
and later forgetful but still
thoughtful and not
forgiven if straying and not
demanding and not overly
curious but helpful
generous of intellect able
to share an idea to endure
pettiness as though it were
not the entirety of the
other's soul or to be
confused with a lack of
better intentions. Not
always critical when
discernment were called
for. thoughtful even
prescient toward the other
and not devious or
frightening when it came
to flirtation but not nervous about sexuality.
considerate where one is
repressed or stingy thus
showing allowance for
one's higher states even
when that one can't attain
to them
in short a memory of the
other on a good day
always before one even in
darkness. allowance for
darkness in the other or
the self. forgiveness for
darkness. no forgiveness
for lies of a sexual kind
where deceit is pervasive.
a wish not to be

interrupted at the bath yet
to yield if impetuosity
exceeds privacy in
strength on occasion.
laughter if one is caught
in the act and
embarrassed but laughter
that embraces not
defaces. weakness
tolerated or scolded
depending. second
chances but not thirds.
but look. Look. there one
is at the bar being pressed
against and just because
she is strong with broad
shoulders and need not
fear and because she has
not feared to let herself
be kissed and to return the
kiss after all and to press
back and move her hips
forward before pushing
one away with a
smile does not mean that
the other is there but
rather is home finding the
touch of other
unendurable and the need
to be beautiful only an
indifferent pastime and
is incapable of being
provocative and because
misery is his arrogance in
disguise is alone always
alone and wanting to be

loved so that the other
coming home and
undressing is hateful in his
sight. When his mother
returned from a Broadway
play with his new father
her horrible dapper
husband who would beat
her that night the
moments before she
unzipped her dress and
reached to release her bra
were fragrant as funerals.
and in the morning the
black and yellow bordered
Playbill would be on the
kitchen counter with the
bold letters of the latest,
Funny Girl, or *Stop the
World I want to Get Off*.

Hands on the Table, Cundiff

What if I took your hands from your table
and held them to my chest
to where that whore of a heart sleeps?
If I wanted each hand on my breasts,
would you listen past skin or ribs for that beating?
What if I made you wait for once
instead of being always available,
your fucking texts after a drink, you impossible ass,
that you send and
I walk away from the wood of the table that
suddenly has a texture I didn't notice before.
And I forget and say out loud, *don't answer him*,
and another man's children look up,

their hair as messy as mine,
and say, *what*?

What if I told you the heat print on your stone floor from
    your bare foot is what I love most
about your body.
That means you are still alive,
still translucent in breath,
bone and pain, not yet ready
for quiet dead stillness
like those lakes in the scary movies you know not to swim in
even if you are a lake girl.

Thoughts have weight in our chests,
ice cold chests,
thinking about how death is heavy,
skin gets hard when we die.
Hard because whatever gases fill up
our skin, when we are put out flat,
for the living to come see,
for the warm to touch
our cold skin and wonder
when it is our turn to lie here
who will come touch our arms?
think how we could have been better.

Bird, Schreiner

That long night at the end of summer
when there was no end of kissing you
you'd turn away, deflecting nothing.
I'd drag you back
as though our mouths were magnets.
You did not seem weary or absorbed
as in time perhaps you would
but were changed by what we did
yet still waiting. It was not to be.

And now it is winter the coldest days
the bright, slightly impaired sunshine
the icy remnants of snow

Standing in a field the herd of buffalo
the road curves and banks
the mill shut down
the Bird Refuge closed only the staff
permitted on its road glazed slick
From inside a cage a woman
angry that I have come past the warning
at the top of the hill
tells me to go back the way I came
do not stop or you will slide back down.
Wild and wary, like her birds, she never appeared.

You'd turn, deflecting nothing.
I'd follow like a magnet
and you'd turn back.

What is a snowy road, and a wild bird,
compared to that?

Easter, 1980, Cundiff

The man next door is shoveling snow too,
his and my breath in sync, grey in the air.
we both push out a clean line,
stand, and then look about nowhere

Now I know why my father
put me on the tractor on Saturdays
instead of dropping me at the Queeny park pool with the

tanned girls.
Instead the gun, heavy in my hand, my shoulder on one side
    growing stronger.
How, I don't know, I lived a childhood in fields and with the
    smell
of oil and knowing the names of tools,
the braying of my beagle at the grey fur of rabbits

Once the beagles got into a rabbit burrow in our backyard
by the neglected woodpile south of the plot.
The babies were half alive still, even after two forty pound
    males were at them.
My father told my brothers, just boys then,
to take a large rock to the newborns,
large in the boys' adolescent hands, we had casually
walked past it one hundred times.
They lifted the rock,
one after the other.
I guess that was worse than hitting.
The punch sound.
I watched from the wide brown window.
Do you know that rabbits scream?

I had the luxury once of running away from love,
luxurious self-touching.
I drove to see his old place last November. I wanted to kneel
    in his grass.
As though there was anything else anywhere ever that would
    feel like a good man's goodness.
There's nothing that good.
Except for maybe loving babies.
People die before we get the chance to make things right. It
    is that simple.

Last night I dreamt of serving him his coffee again.
He looked up, his sockets now gaunt and rimmed in red,
his mouth endless black.
Is this what 38 is?

We get older and accept less.

Go backwards.
Why didn't I run to my brothers,
stop the rock?
I was so skinny, if I had tried,
I would have dangled from their flannelled arms.

Snapshot, Schreiner

A woman takes off her earrings
Preparing to make love. The cold room
Stings for a minute and in the candle
The saints flicker and dance. To think
Moments ago they were dressed and standing
Before a bookshelf. She took down the Fagles
Translation to look for her favorite passage,
Hera seducing Zeus, drugging him, putting on
Her armor and going killing.

Because I couldn't believe in a future for us, Schreiner

doesn't mean I'm not hard at the sink
I lean against. Listening to you for an hour, I mean
talking to you, talking inside your mouth, taking
possession of your words, drawing a blade
across your tongue, tasting your blood there,
seeing it cross that channel where your lips
brush against your teeth like the rain
streams down the side of a smooth white house,
looking at you sideways, that smile almost as wild
as your hair. Then to see how you have turned
sideways on the sofa so that I can see
your collarbone, your shoulders, a necklace you wear

at your timid throat, a pulse there, then the lips
I have filled with my own words, not too
forcefully I hope, pushing against the tension
of your tongue, lining them up like your teeth
in order and among them the witnesses
to my assault there. Then your words come back
and they go against me in the kitchen as it thunders
distant as your neighborhood from mine
so that I know of it, and I think someone must anticipate
a rain about to fall on her drowned garden,
and then you are where you were once before
with your back against my sink, the window framing
the evening into which your sigh escaped,
and I am coming at you and you are
not turning away.

Cliff, Schreiner

>Is your month alone at its end?
>How do you stand there at night
>In your kitchen, in your body
>As you move through the house
>Not yet accustomed to the lights
>You turned on when you walked in

So that the rooms feel violated
And interrupted. You want another
Glass of wine. You've been where you have been
These many nights of late. You kick off
Your shoes, take down your tired dress
Not for the first time this evening
And maybe you think about calling
Someone you love. You go near
The bed but its edge is like the edge
Of a seacliff. You feel the beating of a sea
Down below. It rushes against the cliffs.
They are stony and not resilient
Unlike what you find when you reach
For yourself.

Bookshelf, Cundiff

I'm alone for a month
don't know how you do it.
Walking by a book, you pull it off the shelf.
Open to a page, drop your finger down the lines of ink,
pausing, remembering another state,
a woman's hands around your neck,
her smile before kissing you
before you put it back again.

Dust, Schreiner

You have been so consistent
in your praise
                that it has been difficult
to know what I crave. You have commended
again and again these hands
though they are made of dust
these words though they build the fictions

I have made of my life
and told to you through the glass
the hours of wine
This face is the side of a building
you have driven past in your youth
with your father at the wheel
and your brother ignoring you
Still, you recall where you were being taken
and what it would taste like
when you got there
so are the turns memory takes
and the moments it makes real as a summer
night is real, now, with rain stopping
birds beginning again but only the ones that cry
I don't know if you are there
if you are wearing a shirt
or if you are reaching across the counter
for the knife as you prepare dinner
or raising the wine to your mouth
if the dogs are restless
if you have put them out
if it is three nights more
until your children return
if you are in any kind of mood
of the kind you were in when you dressed
for me one night
o how you offered what you wore
o the terrible settling for nothing
with which I have made peace

Dust II, Cundiff

Like Eurycleia,
I would take each of your fingers to my mouth
and run each tip over my lips,
feeling for each scar

as you spoke of
the cat having slipped away again
or the boar hunt.

There's nothing grand about it.
No monument or tradition that can hold
the small everyday gestures. The bringing of coffee,
The laugh from across the house,
the errand for cough syrup. These sorts of things.
I won't let the porticos and pillars scare me.

It's about the way I understand your voice now.
Your deliberate walking.
The ease of words you make in sentences
strung together casually, like those strings of
summer lights my mother's long white arms lifted
between the two birches on Lering Drive.

Or maybe the most frightening is that
even through the terrible nothing,
that I would love you, still,
despite the dust in the corners or
in your tears, your ruin,
if it meant I would be able to watch you sleep.
Just wondering quietly where you went,
your chest turned away under those sheets
after you had slowed to let me unbutton a shirt
that held, still, in the cotton, the warmth from your skin.

You Came Back, Cundiff

The trail of the veins on your hands
came back when I followed
the black dog into the Ozark forest
to find that a tree's angled climb
from the earth looks just deliberate enough
to resemble a man's hand
bending to write on paper.

Your chest came back
when I stood starboard to the boat
whose motor cut out so its solid draft could
ease a slow straight line into the slip.
"Watch yourself," my father said.
He was right.
Your mind can't drift away around water like that.

That afternoon on the dock,
the sun still pressing into the low skin on my back,
he said, "grip the rope off the side,
hold tight."
So I leaned back and pulled the fraying tendons
hard against my hip.
The golden cording
intimate with me suddenly,
all the hands that had held it before, against all the thighs,
the marine line puckering my skin,
sunburned,
made your arm come back
when against my thigh I saw my skin
bow to permit your weight.

Then lastly, sweeping the porch
after dinner,
the mayflies dancing in the corners
while from inside the sound of the water at the sink
muffled voices,
your mouth came
when I bumped the All-Spice tree.
The thousand milky blooms,
suddenly, deliberately shook off your breath.
Cardamom, cinnamon, and your clove
on a sturdy bed in low light,
where your lips were parted,
and parted near the space below
my navel.
Plantae aromaticum, they call it.

The Authors

Allison Cundiff

ALLISON CUNDIFF is a graduate of Truman State University (BA English Literature) and the University of Missouri (MA in English Literature). Her previous publications include articles in *The Pragmatic Buddhist* and *Feminist Teacher*. She lives in St. Louis.

Steven Schreiner

STEVEN SCHREINER teaches at the University of Missouri-St. Louis. He is the author of *Out of Egypt* (2014) and *Too Soon to Leave*, and the founding editor of *Natural Bridge*, a journal of contemporary literature.

www.ingramcontent.com/pod-product-compliance
Lightning Source LLC
Chambersburg PA
CBHW052109070526
44584CB00017B/2410